D0230034

OPEN WIDE!

WAYLAND

NEW EXPERIENCES

I Want That Room! – Moving house
I'm Still Important! – A new baby
Open Wide! – My first trip to the dentist
Where's My Peg? – My first day at school

First published in 1999 by Wayland Publishers Ltd,
61 Western Road, Hove, East Sussex BN3 1JD, England
© Copyright 1999 Wayland Publishers Limited

Editor: Jason Hook
Designer: Tessa Barwick

British Library Cataloguing in Publication Data
Green, Jen, 1955–
    Open Wide!: My first trip to the dentist. – (New
    experiences)
    1. Dental clinics – Juvenile literature 2. Dentistry –
    Juvenile literature
    I. Title II. Gordon, Mike, 1948–
    617.6

ISBN 0 7502 2504 1

Printed and bound in Italy by G. Canale & C.Sp.A, Turin

OPEN WIDE!

My first trip to the dentist

Written by Jen Green

Illustrated by Mike Gordon

WAYLAND

Oliver is my big brother. One day, he had a toothache. Mum said it was time to go to the dentist.

Mum rang the dentist, and booked a time for me to go as well.

It was my first trip to the dentist. 'What will it be like?' I asked.

'Mr Rose is very gentle,' Mum said.
'He has a special chair that goes up
and down. But you'll have to open
your mouth wide.'

Oliver and I practised sitting
in the big armchair, and
opening our mouths wide.

The next morning, before we went to the dentist, Mum helped us give our teeth a special clean.

Dad took us to the dentist. We sat in the waiting room, where there were toys and comics. I felt a bit worried.

Then the nurse called my name. I held Dad's hand, and we went in.

Kate first, please.

11

'Hello Kate, I'm Mr Rose,' said
the dentist. 'Come and sit on my
special chair.'

Nurse Jenny put a bib around my neck. 'Open wide!' said the dentist. Then he used a mirror and a tool called a probe to check my teeth.

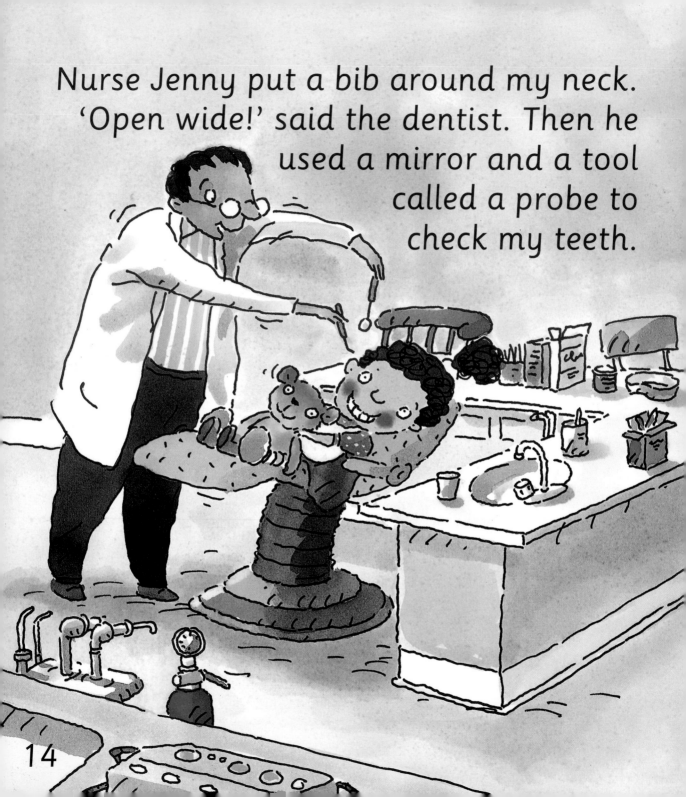

Mr Rose looked pleased. 'Your teeth are fine, Kate. Now I'll give them a special clean.'

The dentist brushed my teeth
with a machine that made
a buzzing sound.

16

It tickled, but it didn't hurt. 'Now rinse out,' said Mr Rose. I rinsed my mouth into a little bowl by the chair.

Dad and I went back to the waiting room. Now it was Oliver's turn.

I looked at a poster which showed how germs from food get stuck in your teeth if you don't brush properly.

Oliver came back, looking very happy. 'The dentist found a hole in the tooth that hurt,' he said.

He opened his mouth, and showed us a silver filling in his tooth.

'Mr Rose gave me an injection. It stung for a second, then my mouth went to sleep. He drilled away the bad part of the tooth.'

'Then he filled the hole with a filling mixed by Nurse Jenny. Now my tooth is good as new,' said Oliver.

Mr Rose called us back in. He showed us how to brush both the inside and the outside of our teeth.

Nurse Jenny gave us each a new
toothbrush. She said: 'Give your teeth
a good brushing, especially at night.'

'Fruit and vegetables, milk and cheese are good for young teeth,' said Mr Rose. 'Too many sweets are not so good.'

26

'What if we get hungry?' asked Oliver. 'Have a healthy snack,' said Nurse Jenny.

At the desk we booked our next trip to the dentist. 'See you in six months,' said Nurse Jenny.

Mum was waiting for us at home. 'The dentist gave me a toothbrush!' I told her. 'And I opened my mouth very wide!'

Notes for parents and teachers

This book introduces children to the subjects of going to the dentist and looking after teeth. Parents and teachers may find it useful to stop and discuss issues as they come up in the book.

Have children visited the dentist yet? If they have, encourage them to discuss their own experiences, talking about their feelings as well as what happened. Common experiences at the dentist include having an X-ray taken, having a brace fitted to straighten teeth, and having a damaged or decayed tooth removed.

Reread the story, encouraging children to act out the roles of different characters. Children might like to make up a story about a trip to the dentist, using the book as a framework. The story could be based on real or imaginary experiences. Individual stories could be put together to make a play about a day at the dentist's surgery, with children taking turns to play themselves and the surgery staff.

Make a list of all the new words and terms associated with a visit to the dentist, including – waiting room, probe, germs, filling, drill, injection. Discuss what the words mean. Children might like to make a list of all the tools the dentist uses, or compose a shopping list of things a dentist's surgery might need to replace at the end of a busy week. They could also make a list of all the things we use our teeth for, for example talking as well as eating.

What would life be like without teeth? Introduce the fact that some people are fitted with a false tooth or a whole set of false teeth.

Explain the importance of having regular check-ups at the dentist, and of brushing teeth thoroughly, the backs as well as the fronts, especially at bedtime. Using the text on pages 18–19, discuss plaque – a layer of left-over food and germs that forms on teeth, particularly around gums, and causes tooth decay. You could highlight the problem of plaque by using plaque-disclosing tablets, available from chemists. Remind children to brush really well in the areas where plaque forms.

Use this book for teaching literacy

This book can help you in the literacy hour in the following ways:

- ✓ Children can write simple stories linked to personal experience, using the language of the text in this book as a model for their own writing. (Year 1, Term 3: Non-fiction writing composition.)
- ✓ Children can look through the book and try to locate verbs with past and present tense endings. (Year 1, Term 3: Word recognition, graphic knowledge and spelling.)
- ✓ The use of speech bubbles shows a different way of presenting text. (Year 2, Term 2: Sentence construction and punctuation.)

Books to read

A Day in the Life of a Dentist by Carol Watson (Franklin Watts, 1997). Ravi and Ailsa are dentists. The book tells the story of all the patients they see in the course of a busy day. Ravi's morning is going smoothly when he is interrupted by an emergency patient, Ojay, whose tooth has been knocked out.

Let's Talk About Going to the Dentist by Marianne Johnston (Heinemann, 1997). This book describes what to expect on a visit to the dentist, and explains the uses of all the tools you see at the dentist's surgery.

Usborne First Experiences: Going to the Dentist by Anne Civardi and Stephen Cartwright (Usborne Publishing, 1992). Jake and Jessie take a trip to the dentist, and learn all about how to look after their teeth.